Ulick O'Connor

POEMS

of the

DAMNED

CHARLES BAUDELAIRE'S

Les Fleurs du Mal —The Flowers of Evil

Monarchline / Wolfhound Press

Published by Monarchline, an imprint of Wolfhound Press Ltd
68 Mountjoy Square, Dublin 1

ISBN 0 86327 512 5

A catalogue-in-publication entry
is available from The British Library

First published 1995

The author and publisher acknowledge the assistance of
the cultural department of the French Embassy,
Alliance Française, towards the publication of the volume.

Wolfhound Press receives financial assistance from
The Arts Council, An Chomhairle Ealaíon.

Cover illustration © John Kelly, R.H.A.
Cover design Joe Gervin
Book design and layout Wolfhound Press
Printed in the Republic of Ireland by Colour Books, Dublin

Contents

Preface

Introduction

Michel Déon, de l'Académie Française

POEMS OF THE DAMNED

Ulick O'Connor is a biographer, poet and playwright. He has published three books of poems: *Lifestyles* (1975), *All Things Counter* (1986) and *One is Animate* (1990). He is well known for his verse plays in the Noh form which were first produced at the Abbey Theatre in 1977 and later during the Dublin Theatre Festival in 1979, going into an off-Broadway production in 1981. His play *Executions* broke attendance records when it was produced at the Abbey Theatre in Autumn 1985, while two years later, *A Trinity of Two* – which dealt with Edward Carson and Oscar Wilde – had a similar success. His one-man play *Joyicity,* first presented at the Abbey, was an instant success at the Dublin Theatre and Edinburgh Festivals, and enjoyed a packed off-Broadway run in January 1991. He is a member of Aosdána and is on its Toscaireacht (Executive).

Michel Déon (born 1919 in Paris) is a French writer and playwright who, after many years living in Italy, Portugal and Greece, has settled in Ireland. Author of many novels and essays, among which is *A Purple Taxi* (made into a film shot in Ireland), he is a member of the Académie Française (1978), of the Academia de Lisboa and *doctor honoris causa* of the National University of Ireland.

Preface

In April 1855, eighteen poems by Charles Baudelaire appeared in the *Revue des Deux Mondes*. The title he gave this collection was *Les Fleurs du Mal*. These poems caused a sensation for their outspoken themes and frank images. When *Les Fleurs du Mal* was later published in an extended version, Baudelaire was prosecuted for obscenity by the French Courts and copies of his book were confiscated. Two of the banned poems, 'The Damned Women' and 'Lethe', are included here. The ban on the prohibited poems was not lifted until May 1949 by the French Court of Appeals.

The year 1995 is the one hundred and fortieth anniversary of the publication of Baudelaire's poems in the *Revue des Deux Mondes*. Ulick O'Connor commemorates the anniversary with eighteen poems selected from *Les Fleurs du Mal*.

Introduction
MICHEL DÉON
de l'Académie Française

Jean Cocteau said 'What is poetry? Nobody knows, but the whole world knows that we cannot live without it.' It is, in essence, mysterious, like an encrypted language in which figures are hidden behind words and their rhythm. One's taste in poetry is very individual. The admirer of Victor Hugo has nothing in common with the enthusiast of Mallarmé, yet even across centuries of time Villon and Apollinaire seem to go hand in hand. Baudelaire is unique in that he has a universal appeal. He is at once open and secretive. He who discovers him never forgets. At a particular moment in all our lives he is our poet. We can, thereafter, be attracted by other chants but we can never forget the intoxicating pleasure that he aroused in us that day when we were hungry and thirsty, when we needed someone to talk to us of tenderness and of pity, of horror and also of beauty.

Charles Baudelaire is a poet so quintessentially French that I could never imagine his unique magic being successfully translated into another language. Would we still hear his voice so proud and yet so plaintive? Ulick O'Connor dared carry out this most delicate of tasks and, with a success that is rare, he has managed to produce the most unlikely of renderings in an English which is both sensual and earthy and which actually re-invents the French verse. He is both faithful and unfaithful to the original work, he has, by some miracle, managed to preserve the familiar Baudelairian cadence. His rhythm has such a natural grace that one is bewitched by it. The poem is reborn before our very eyes and is music to our ears, not translated but recreated.

When I read, in *'La Géante'* ('The Giantess'):

Devinir si son coeur couve une sombre flamme
Aux humides brouillards qui nagent dans ses yeux...

and I find the ellipsis and the idea marvellously inversed:

And from the mists which round her eyes would swirl,
Muse, if her heart nourished some tragic flame...

I applaud the achievement. Everything is there. What more can I say?

In the last verse of *'Tristesse de la lune'* ('Sorrows of the Moon'): *'Et la met dans son coeur loin des yeux du soleil...'* an abridged version appears: 'To treasure in his heart far from the sun's eyes....' – I am rendered speechless. The poet O'Connor offers to the poet Baudelaire an unparalleled 'treasure'.

Valery Larbaud, who dedicated so much of his time and his genius to foreign literature and who was responsible for introducing Joyce into France, places such translators in the care of Saint Jerome, their protector, inspirer and friend. It would indeed take no less than a saint to protect and thank them adequately. Self-effacement and the giving of self are the two principal commandments of the translator. Poetry rarely has the chance to be so honoured and served in its spirit as well as in its form.

Extracts from unfinished draft prefaces which Baudelaire planned for editions of *Les Fleurs du Mal.*

Poetry touches music through prosody
whose roots go deeper into the human soul than any
classical theory can demonstrate.

A poet who is incapable of appreciating the number of rhymes
a word may have is incapable of expressing any idea whatever.

Rhyme and rhythm satisfy man's immortal need for monotony,
symmetry and surprise.

My book may have done some good; I am not grieving over that.
It may have done some harm; I am not rejoicing over that.

Every crime I have recounted has been attributed to me.

The poet is of no persuasion. Otherwise, he would be a mere
mortal.

It is more difficult to love God than to believe in Him.
However, it is more difficult for people today
to believe in the Devil than to love him.

The Giantess

In that age when nature with her powerful pulse
Would each day some prodigious child bear fruit,
I would have loved to have lived close to a young giantess,
Like a voluptuous cat lying at a queen's foot.

I would have watched her body flower like her soul,
Expanding famously at her mighty game;
And from the mists which round her eyes would swirl,
Muse, if her heart nourished some tragic flame:

To explore those splendid contours at my ease;
Negotiate the slopes of those enormous knees;
And in the summer, when the malign sun would keep

Her stretched across the fields prone in heat,
In the shadow of her breasts nonchalantly to sleep,
Like a peaceful hamlet at the mountain's feet.

Glad To Be Dead

Deep in slimy earth surrounded by snails
I want to dig myself a gaping pit,
Where like a shark in a wave, snug beyond gales
I can stretch my creaking bones a little bit.

I hate tombs, legacies, those sort of shows
Rather than ask for some sign of remorse
By staying alive, I would prefer to ask the crows
To lap the blood from my loathsome corpse.

Worms without ears or eyes, to your dark company
Admit now a new friend, joyous and free
As for you prosperous philosophers, sons of filth,

Across my tomb step without remorse or dread,
Let me know if you find some new torment built
For this dogsbody without soul among the dead.

Sorrows Of The Moon

How lazily to-night the moon dreams above the land;
Like a rare beauty on her cushioned couch,
Who before she slips to sleep allows her hand
Caress her breast, with slight and sensuous touch.

On the satined back of soft drifts of foam
Swooning, she reclines, as night flies by,
Lifting her eyes towards those shapes that roam
Like flowers, the floating terraces of the sky.

When sometimes the languid one lets fall
On earth just one furtive tear, that's all,
A pious poet, disdainful of sleep's prize,

Will cradle that pale tear within his hand
With its reflecting irises like a diamond band
To treasure in his heart, far from the sun's eyes.

The Rebel

An Angel swoops like an eagle from the firmament,
Grabs the miscreant's hair in his strong fist
And shaking it says 'There is just one Commandment.
(See here I am your good Angel) I must insist!

'You'll learn to love with no hint of distaste,
The poor, wicked, the stupid, that whole dazed forum,
So that for Jesus, when He comes, you will have placed
The triumphant carpet of your love before Him.

'This is charity. Before your heart grows cold,
Rekindle your ecstasy within His fold,
That true voluptuousness whose charm won't fade away.'

The Angel chastising, as he would (indeed) love
The blasphemer, pummels him with giant fists from above;
But the damned one answers always 'I will not obey.'

The Cat

Within my head there perambulates,
As if in his own apartment,
This gorgeous cat, strong and with refinement,
You scarcely hear his purr as it vibrates.

The tone is so tender so laid back,
Whether his voice soothes or scolds,
With resonance and depth it rolls
This is his secret, his real knack.

This voice, which pearls and flows
To the dark corners of my mind,
Pulses in me like a poem, I find
I'm spellbound, my being glows.

His sound can calm the most cruel hurt
Imbued with such soothing prescience.
It can suggest the longest sentence
Without ever having to use a word.

There is no bow which can wing
My heart, that most perfect instrument,
And have it quiver with such sentiment,
It rings like music on a throbbing string,

As your voice, mysterious cat,
Which is like that of an angel
In which harmony and sweetness mingle
Exotic, seraphic, yes. I may call you that.

From his fur, white and russet-brown,
Proceeds so sweet a perfume
That from his kiss alone, I almost swoon,
Just one caress and I am undone.

He is the real owner of this pad,
He judges, he presides, to inspire
Everything here as his own empire,
Surely he is some spirit or a god.

When my eyes are drawn to this feline elf
As they would be to a lover,
He returns my gaze, careless what I discover
And what do I find there, I find myself.

I gaze with wonder and my caution shrinks
Under the fire of those pale pupils,
Those clear lanterns and twilight jewels
That contemplate me firmly without a blink.

Don Juan In Hell
(after 'The Impenitent' by Delacroix)

When Don Juan descended to the stream below
He first of all to Charon paid his fees,
A swarthy beggar took the oars to row
With cruel and powerful arms, proud as Antisthenes.

Dishevelled gowns displaying their drooping breasts,
Women writhing under a tumultuous sky
Like a great herd of sacrificial beasts,
Trail behind him with a continual cry.

Laughing Sganarelle comes to claim his wages,
While Don Luis with quavering hand declares
To all the dead who gather at these edges,
This is the blackguard son who mocked his silver hairs.

The chaste Elvira shivering and thin, meanwhile
Faces the treacherous spouse she once adored,
To win from him just one last supreme smile
Such as lit his face when first he pledged his word.

Cased in armour, a huge stone man on board,
Seizes the helm and navigates the Sound.
But our cool hero, leaning upon his sword,
Watches only the wake's foam, scorning to look around.

The Albatross

Often to amuse themselves, the sailors catch
The albatross, giant creatures of the sky,
Indolent companions of the voyage who watch
The white ships on the bitter foam glide by.

Hardly have they hauled their captive through the rail
Than these sky-kings, clumsy now and shamed,
Begin to let their great wings droop and trail
Like oars beside them, pitiably tamed.

Winged voyager, how feeble you've become,
Lately so lovely, ugly once on board.
With his pipe a sailor goads the beak that's dumb;
Another limping, mocks the cripple who once soared.

The poet resembles these princes of the clouds,
Daring the tempest and the hunter's slings.
Exiled on earth amid the jeers of crowds,
His movement impeded by his giant wings.

Icarus' Lament

The lovers of prostitutes
Are satisfied, awoken.
Look at me, arms broken
Hugging clouds as substitutes.

Those fantastic stars, the ones
Which blaze from the skies' depth,
Have blinded me till I am left
With only memories of suns.

I've tried to estimate
In space, where end and centre lie.
Beneath an unknown burning eye
My wings melt and disintegrate.

Burned by the beauty I crave,
I don't have the sublime bliss
Of putting my name on that abyss,
Which will serve as my grave.

Little Old Ladies (III)

Little old ladies, how often have I followed them!
Especially one who, as the dying sun departs
And vermilion wounds bloody the evening's rim,
Would sit on a park bench, pensive and apart,

Delighting in those concerts with their ringing brass
With which the army sometimes grace our parks,
Making us feel reborn as the golden evenings pass
And some heroism pours into people's hearts.

Her, I recall still, proud, with a queen's stance,
Absorbed in the valour of some martial quarrel.
Sometimes her eye would open with an eagle glance,
The marble forehead lifted for the laurel.

The End Of The Day

Beneath a thin sun
Life writhes without reason
Moves shamelessly, runs,
Till on the horizon

Comes sensuous night,
And as hunger eases
Shame takes its flight,
The poet says 'Oh Jesus

My spirits oppress me,
My back cries for respite,
Though dark dreams enmesh me

I will roll with delight
In the curtains of night,
Whose shades will refresh me.'

The Ransom

Man, to pay his ransom,
Has two rich fields of soil
Where he must plough and toil
With the blade of reason.

For the smallest rose to grow,
To extract some ears of corn,
The water must be drawn
From the sweat of his grey brow.

One is Art, the other Love,
Which the Judge will adjudicate
On that awful day of fate
When he will arrive from above.

There must be at his disposal
Full barns and luscious flowers
Whose colours and contours
Will win the Angels' approval.

The Damned Women
(Delphine and Hippolyte)

In the white clearness of the lamp's last hiss,
On cushions soaked in scent with beating heart,
Hippolyte dreamed of that tremendous kiss
Which tore the veil of her innocence apart.

She searches now with tempest troubled eyes
The receding sky of the simplicity she'd lost,
Like a traveller who turns his head and sighs
For blue horizons, which that morning he had crossed.

Her tired eyes, her languid tears, her frown
And dazed air, superb voluptuousness,
Her limp arms thrown like futile weapons down,
Served only to enhance her frail loveliness.

Stretched at her feet, contented now and gay,
Delphine devours her with shining eyes;
Like a savage beast who contemplates its prey,
Having with its teeth, first marked the prize.

Strong beauty, before frail beauty superbly kneels,
Breathing sensuously the wine of victory,
Leaning towards her love, she hopes to win
Some sweet token of their ecstasy.

Delphine seeks in her pale victim's eye
The silent hymn aroused on pleasure's fields,
Which flutters the eyelids after a prolonged sigh
In sublime thanksgiving for the gift she yields.

'Hippolyte, dear heart, can I now assume
That you will not submit in any way,
The sacred sacrifice of your first roses' bloom
To violent gusts, which will wither them away.

'My kisses are like tiny flies that flit
And caress at evening the glass face of lakes;
Not those of one who'd carve a cruel rut
Like the furrow which the brutal ploughshare makes;

'Man will trample you like a savage herd
Of horse or cattle with pitiless hooves,
Hippolyte, my sister, can you not speak one word;
My soul, my heart, my half of me, all that I choose.

'Grant from blue eyes glowing like stars at night;
Just one bewitching look that you may send,
And I shall lift the veil on still more rare delights,
Lull you to sleep in dreams that have no end!'

Hippolyte now raised her young head from the shade.
'Call me not ungrateful, nor do I regret in the least
What we have done my Delphine; but I am troubled and afraid
As if it was the night after some fearful feast.

'Swooping down on me I feel a frightful load;
Black ranks marching, a host of phantoms without shape
Trying to lure me, along a shifting road
Towards a bleeding sky from which there's no escape.

'Have we then committed some dreadful sin
How else explain this terror which endures
When you say "My Angel" I tremble within
Yet my lips are relentlessly drawn to yours.

'Don't look at me like that, sister of my choice;
You whom I love forever and for whom,
Even if you've set a snare, I still rejoice,
Though it may be the commencement of my doom.'

Delphine, tossing her tragic mane,
And like a goddess from her plinth above,
Trembling in prophecy, makes her daring claim;
'Who speaks of hell before the power of love?

'A curse on that useless dreamer who first thought,
When faced with love's inexplicable laws,
That he could solve the mystery if he sought
To mix some honour with its anarchic cause.

'Who seeks to unify in mystic kin
Shade and light, day with the night above,
Will never warm his paralytic skin
With that scarlet sun, we give the name of Love!

'Go find some stupid oaf among the pack;
Deliver your virgin heart to his cruel clutch;
Then pale with horror and remorse come back
And show me your breasts savaged by his touch.

'One can only serve one master of the heart,'
But the girl burst out in a sudden shriek of pain;
'I feel as if I am being ripped apart,
Some gaping abyss where love once has lain.

'Burning like a volcano nothing can withstand
This groaning monster, whose will must have its way
Or quench the Fury's thirst, waving in her hand
A flaming torch to burn my blood away.

'Since between the world and us a curtain must exist,
In that languor, which will penetrate this room,
I annihilate myself upon your breasts
And there discover the freshness of the tomb!'

Descend unhappy victims and begin
That infernal voyage, where you will be hurled
Into the deepest pit, and all your sins
Scourged by a wind which is not of this world.

      .   .   .

Far from the living and condemned to roam,
You race like wolves across the desert shelf;
Disordered souls, seeking a fate that is your own,
While ignoring the divinity within yourself!

The Owls

Black yews shelter them as they wait
Owls perched aloft in regular rows.
Like strange gods they view the world below,
Red eyes flashing, and meditate.

Motionless they occupy this space,
Until that melancholy hour will come,
When thrusting down the sliding sun
The shadows will resume their regular place.

From such the wise become aware
That if we don't accept things as they are,
Shun the tumult and the movement,

Obsessed with what is and what is not;
We must shoulder our own punishment
For having wished to change our lot.

Lethe

Rest on my heart, cruel and sullen one.
Adored tigress, monster of indolent air,
I long in the thickness of your tawny hair,
To plunge my trembling fingers till I'm done.

To bury the burden of my aching head
In the perfume of your towering skirts,
Like a withered flower, to savour though it hurts
The sweet odour of a love that's dead.

Rather than live, for sleep my body longs
To slip into a slumber sweet as death.
I shower remorselessly kisses with each breath
Upon your body with its gleam of bronze.

Nothing can equal your bed's abyss
To engulf and soothe my bitter cries,
On those lips deep oblivion lies,
And all Lethe surges through your kiss.

From now on I shall act as Fate requires,
And use the unhappiness from which it stemmed,
A willing martyr and innocent condemned,
Who fuels his agony with his own desires.

I shall drink to drown my rancour for a start,
Nectar, sweet hemlock and the rest
From the ravishing tips of your erect breast
Which never once has held a captive heart.

The Enemy

My youth was nothing but a darkening storm
Enlivened now and then by brilliant suns;
But rain and thunder shaped a different form
And few fresh flowers survive the withered ones.

Now that I have reached the autumn of the mind,
I must find work for every rake and spade
To clear the flooded land and leave behind
New pastures, where tomb-like pits are laid.

Who knows if the flowers of which I dream
Will find fresh soil on this new shore swept clean,
Some mystic power, from which another life can start.

Ah, the pity of it; time diverts life's flood
And that secret enemy which devours the heart
Sustains itself upon our bartered blood.

The Passerby

My ears deafened in the street's mayhem:
A woman in full mourning passes by
Majestic, sad, a languid hand held high,
Lifting and balancing the borders of her hem.

Noble, statuesque in limb, you sense her power;
My mind on fire I see behind her eye
Some tempest trembling in a livid sky,
Softnesses which bewitch, pleasures which devour.

A flash of lightning – night – beauty fled
In whose glance I have been suddenly reborn
Shall I see you in another world instead?

Elsewhere; perhaps never; condemned to mourn
I know not where you fled – or you not where I go
You whom I could have loved – you who knew it so.

The Wine of Lovers

What a space we have today;
No bridle, bit, or spur to stay
Our rapture; as we roam the sky
Wine as our horse, you and I.

Like two reckless angels driven
By a fevered sea towards heaven,
In the crystal blue of morning
Follow the mirage that's forming.

Balanced gently on the wings
Of friendly whirlwinds let us glide,
Share the delirium that it brings.

My sister, swimming side by side,
We'll skim the surface till it seems
We've reached the Eden of my dreams.

Meditation

Oh Sorrow mine, be wise and unafraid
You longed for evening; see it falls out there
The fading light softening the city's shade,
Bringing peace to some and to others care.

While that vile crew, driven by Pleasure's whip
The cruel torturer, must reap remorse
In slavish feasts; oh Sorrow mine, slip
Your hand in mine; and seek some other source

Far from here. See in torn robes the lost years
Lean from the skies' balconies while Regret appears
Smiling from the waves, as evening pales.

The dying sun slips down beneath an arch
And from the Eastern sky a long shroud trails.
Hold, beloved, hold, sweet Night is on the march.

Other books by Ulick O'Connor

BIOGRAPHY
Biographers & the Art of Biography
(Wolfhound Press)
Brendan Behan
Celtic Dawn: A Portrait of the Irish Literary Renaissance
Oliver St. John Gogarty

PLAYS & POETRY
Three Noh Plays, (Wolfhound Press)
Lifestyles
All Things Counter
One is Animate
Executions

OTHER BOOKS
Irish Tales & Sagas
A Critic at Large
The Campbell Companion (with memoir)
The Yeats Companion (with memoir)
Sport is My Lifeline
The Troubles (Ireland 1912-22)

Wolfhound Press, 68 Mountjoy Square, Dublin 1.
Tel: 874 0354. Fax: 872 0207
Write or telephone for our complete catalogue.